green girl dreams Mountains

green girl
dreams Mountains

by

Marilyn Dumont

OOLICHAN BOOKS
LANTZVILLE, BRITISH COLUMBIA, CANADA
2001

Canadian Cataloguing in Publication Data

Dumont, Marilyn
       green girl dreams mountains

       Poems
       ISBN 0-88982-200-X

       I. Title.
PS8557.U53633G73 2001   C813'.54   C2001-910513-4
PR9199.3.D8465G73 2001

We gratefully acknowledge the support of the Canada Council for the
Arts for our publishing program.

THE CANADA COUNCIL | LE CONSEIL DES ARTS
FOR THE ARTS | DU CANADA
SINCE 1957 | DEPUIS 1957

Grateful acknowledgement is also made to the BC Ministry of Tourism,
Small Business and Culture for their financial support.

BRITISH
COLUMBIA
ARTS COUNCIL
Supported by the Province of British Columbia

We acknowledge the financial support of the Government of Canada
through the Book Publishing Industry Development Program for our
publishing activities.

Published by
Oolichan Books
P.O. Box 10, Lantzville
British Columbia, Canada
V0R 2H0

Printed in Canada

Dedicated in loving memory to

Mary Dumont
and
Johnny Cardinal

Acknowledgments

Vancouver Poetry Women—
Kate Braid
Sioux Browning
Shauna Paull
Miranda Pearson
Denise Ryan
Esta Spalding

Contents

Homeground

gravity / 13
monuments, cowboys & indians, tin cans, and
red wagons / 14
Mother, Ice Cream, Cigarettes, Newspapers and
Sin / 16
lucky stars / 17
anti-I-over / 19
kindling / 21
mother Church daughter / 22
the dimness of mothers and daughters / 23
yellow bird / 24
replica / 25
the place you left open / 26
jig dream / 27
not Dick & Jane / 28
then came Christmas / 29
house, broken / 30
will I, night / 31
I am five / 32
ghosted / 33
the shape of water / 35

City View

Main & Hastings / 39
Powell / 40
"the drive" / 41
Robson / 42
Napier / 43
Salsbury / 44
Oak / 45
Hastings / 46
Terminal avenue / 47
Broadway / 48

Gazing Ground

grazing grounds / 51
mirage / 52
nothing asks me to leave / 53
The Bow River, Shaganappi, and Sarcee Trails / 54
Wapiti / 55

Mine Fields

green girl dreams Mountains / 59
naked wind / 60
mine fields / 61
having said nothing, yet / 62
burn, blaze now / 65
scorching / 66
lover / 68
pastries / 69
the stain / 70
a sorry slackening / 71
wrapping the bundle of my dream of you / 72

Among the Word Animals

word swarm / 75
solo / 76

sound shard / 77
birdnote / 78
sad flute / 79
stillness for company / 80
still / 81
roll / 82
raw / 83
bright beads / 84
"dawn always begins in the bones" / 85
birds pin it down / 86
I give you arbutus / 87
arbutus I / 88
arbutus II / 89
dried stigmas of crocus / 90
up/write / 91
grammar boot camp / 93
Straw Boss / 94
blond syllables / 95
throatsong to the four-leggeds / 96

Homeground

gravity

my brother wasn't born
he fell from the sky
while I was drying dishes
friction, the only natural law
suspended him for me
through the sound of limbs cracking
their dry rhythm announcing
his delivery to earth
and mom's gasp to see him walk
and flop on the couch
where it seemed he lay
for his adolescence
but through his example
she wouldn't have to repeat herself
her warnings of danger
to this family of falling things

monuments, cowboys & indians, tin cans, and red wagons

We lived at the end of a road
that dissolved into a field
flat as a table and the color of deer;
although I saw no deer there
that field rolled out for miles to a deep cliff
that fell to a river
and that Red Deer River
was our source of water
hauled home by our black dog, Chinnie

and our old school house
jut out of that flatness
like a misplaced monument
to the wanderings home and away
of an extended family of half-breeds
kids scattering to cowboys and indians, tin cans, red wagons
teenagers jiving to Del Shannon
migrating Settlement relatives searching for work
their wives or "old ladies" in tow
and on Saturday nights with two weeks pay
the Silk Tassle, Pilsner, and fiddle tunes would flow
weave through auntie's rank laughter, mom's stepdancing and
my brother's yodelling
Cree would occupy the house like a new code, the partying would
heat up the walls and spill out windows and doors like light
through cracks

And that old school house had long divided windows and
the same paint the school board issued
when my father bought it
the sun's rays a potato peeler
that curled the paint away from the boards
where that field spread out and away from the schoolhouse
like an epic film shot
until the sun sank into the wet field
between the house and river
ending our days like forged steel dipped in water

Mother, Ice Cream, Cigarettes, Newspapers and Sin

It's an overcast, muggy September evening and I'm sitting on the porch enjoying the last of an ice cream cone at age forty, and I think of my mother and how much she likes ice cream, how much she loves to say in a childlike voice, even with her diabetes, "I can have a little cone." I think of how beguiling she can be, so sweet and yet so fierce, how these things can coexist in one person, in one place, in one ice cream cone.

I think of her and realise that I am now her age when she used to sit at the end of her bed at night and smoke two cigarettes. Every night like clockwork, she'd smoke two cigarettes in the dark, then she'd put on her nightgown, wind the clock for the next workday and pray.

Other times she would ask me to go to the store and buy her a pear or banana. And sometimes she would walk to the store herself. But she always returned with more; she'd come back with a hand of bananas, tiny donuts dusted in icing sugar and a newspaper. Always a newspaper.

She loved to sit and read "the paper." Oh, she read other things, like *Woman's Own,* but mostly she loved to kick back in her Lazy-Boy, with an unabashed heave she'd find her angle of repose and hold the paper at arm's length. A supplicant to information. Her head slightly at an angle, her eyes would be glued to all the gory and sordid details of murders, thefts and beatings. The only sound was her occasional muffled gasp at the crimes committed therein. To her, every detail was that sin unfolding before her eyes

lucky stars

many times I am taken back
to my parents in that logging camp
my brother driving
one hand on the wheel, singing
in a voice I grew to envy
his hair slicked back, a ducktail
and me bundled in the back seat
fixed to those big-eyed stars
overhead

so often
I have ignored this memory
of me lying still
in his nest of blankets and pillows
but I didn't know then
how rare mothering was
in a family of ten

but that night I imbibed it
the swaddling, the glowing
my brother's voice
his sweet eyes
watermelon-seed
shiny
in the dashboard light

our high beams splitting
the dark wood ahead;
luck pulling us through
the small cracks

me held up
by one thistle of a star and
my brother's ducktail unfurling
like innocence

anti-I-over

at eight years old, I'd
hurl a ball up into the smooth darkness
of summer night, past the peak of our tar-shingled roof
while my brother waited to predict its fall on the other side
I imagined this fist-sized ball
rising above everything except
wing-ed beings
out of reach of broken things
or rooms where parents
pressed time in their hands
like gods

where these same self-made gods rattled
every board and breath awake
with their suspicions and charges of infidelity
in one another
for all to hear and pull on their shame
like heavy boots
tethering our feet to the ground

instead of lifting like that ball
into the stretching wing-ed place
into that lake on its belly
that my brother and I reached for
higher than any ball we'd ever thrown

to think that that sky stretched
away and near
to someone as small as myself
dwarfed by the walls of our house and
deep night buoyant with promise
delivered by the season's humming
that snapped the light of dream in me
like street lights popping on
our voices bending off a wall or
the sky for all we knew

when the first star lit
like a far off porchlight
those nights belonged to us
our parents had all turned inside
somewhere still
in anticipation of our curfew
and time to make our lunches
wrap bologna sandwiches
and cream-filled cookies
place them all in a paper bag
with an apple the size of that ball

kindling

my mother's handwriting never afforded her the long loping
lines of educated grace. Her letters were crippled, blunt-
fisted and left hanging at the edge of a sentence-fragment
like her language register, in a university classroom
Her "c's" were cramped like fingers holding onto
something too long

Her sentences veered off the page like a drunk
weaving the center line; her "o's" collapsed in on themselves
exhausted; her "m's" tried to claw their way out
while her "l's" and "t's" were left
broken twigs on the page
as kindling
for me

mother Church daughter

not just any mother and daughter
walk purposely
past this Sunday morning, bright
the both of them after
scrubbing for church, for
what other reason would
the spindly girl in red and white
polka dots appear so prideful, long
brown eight-year-old legs sprouting
down from the new dress beside
her mother's resolved, freshly
shampooed determination

the dimness of mothers and daughters

I.

This is a story shaped by you
as big as your words or
as long as your sentences
This is your story
even though you haven't told it
all or don't know how to tell
parts of it yet. By starting the story
the story tells you, tells you how
to go on and how to look back

II.

And
you can look back not
to find a way out
or a way around
but a way through
the dimness of mothers & daughters

III.

Look back over your life like
looking back over a beaded design, accepting
the misplaced, or the misshapen
even misrepresented
Some beads fell
never got stitched in
place, but there was a pattern
there was a plan

yellow bird

call it jaundice or the eventual   in a mother's face but
her light emerged there   in her face   in the bone
thin yellow bird she had become   her face a small moon
still   surprised I had courage enough   to keep looking
I was fixed to her   adored her like pollen
while her body diffused   her limbs, leaving
a pile of twigs   to start a fire

replica

I coaxed you one July morning   to tea and donuts in the
park   your wheelchair a sleeping piece of metal   resisted in
place of you   I believed having you feel the sun on your face
would call you out

We found a spot near a sapling   proud of its limbs   I tried talk
of small worldly things: weather and work   but you were
practiced at drifting inward too long   you were smaller   your
ailments had outgrown both of us   colitis, diabetes, and a
failing liver   made you lose interest in dragging yourself
through days that were just a replica   you no longer attempted
to hide the place you had gone to   your hours were crowded
with life played backwards   till one day something bigger gave
way   your chest sank   your torso curved like a claw around its
own breath   but, even in your absence   some part of your
body-illness remembered pain   the final raking   even when
you were barely there   you had long gone

the place you left open

the place you always told me to close   at the bottom of the
stair   is open to randomness now   yesterday while giving a
poetry reading, I thought of how you spoke Cree   I felt loss
and wondered if I ever would   one night I dreamt of helping
you move   it was one of those dreams where packing my
things blurred with packing yours   I woke the next morning
feeling cold and small   Later I realized I was dreaming of mov-
ing from my place and I was moving you to it   it's when I
think of talking to you and remember you're dead that takes
me aback   the sheerest image though   the cruelest   is the
one of you sitting at the dinner table in palliative care   your
meal untouched in front of you   your head, a heavy broken
bud   dangles from its stalk   one month earlier, you cried
apologetically, "I can't help it, my girl," and I didn't under-
stand what you meant

jig dream

and the dancers kept streaming past   a long line of dancers
kept passing, kept dancing   children dressed in red and white
and metis sashes, black shoes like a phalanx of soldiers,   red
soldiers   and they were many   as far as the eye could see
many   children, many soldiers   feet flying to a fiddle, feet
quick as fish fins light and fast and fleet and   change up change
up   that fiddle and flick of feet   Oh I wanted to dance   wanted
to dance, but I was still   held fast   paralysed by desire and
dread and desire and dread   and I could not lift my knees to
the fiddle, my feet to fiddle, but the children kept dancing and
dancing and I wanted   oh I wanted to show them how I could
jig

not Dick & Jane

a family story
not Dick & Jane, or even Spot
but the dull ache of neglect, rusted
now the colour of dried blood
clasped in the inertness of those we call
relative

brother we share the same
a father who hid in a manly bottle, and
a mother who kept one eye on him
and the other on her suitcase

then came Christmas

"Through the year pain came and went, then came
Christmas, everything correct, everything in order."
Omeros, Derrick Walcott

through the year pain came and went as we opened and closed
our shutters to the world outside our family shame that crested
and fell like waves in our own sea sickness, the pain came like
the flu that held on for two weeks mostly at Christmas, a flu
that came suddenly but expected, the pain that I thought then,
my father brought home, as someone would bring home a stray
cat or dog, and its presence inhabited our house like a heavy
spirit, a spirit that would plague us with chills, feverishness,
sleeplessness and obsessive thinking about the force that would
engulf, consume us if we stopped thinking about it, about try-
ing to control its out-of-controllness, but I would, think con-
tinually, think even while thinking of something else, double
think as if thinking had layers, as if thoughts could be stacked like
chairs in a church hall or layered like blankets, and I would think
of all the ways to stop it, of all the ways I could personally change
it by my behavior, but it happened every year anyway, then Christ-
mas came and everything was not correct, everything was not in
order

house, broken

god where were you when   my father slumped head-swollen
in the soured sun?   when he, sober-sorry, couldn't see me?
when my mother ran and I wandered out to the shocked walls
stained now with curses, bruises and the acrimony of night?
where were you when I called again and again, believing you
would hold the fist of my father and the tongue of my mother?
that you'd make them let go   fall away like dogs   where were
you when the house fell silent and fear rose in me like the sun
wondering which one of them would be left, and   which one
would break free?   I would hate the one that escaped   would
hate her for her leaving   because she could, because she slid
from the cleft that lodged in my breastbone   god where were
you when I moved faint and weightless   in that broken house
and the carcass   held me in its hull   so I wouldn't float away
from this earth?

will I, night

I shy from the familiar in these woods where
I'm alone, here my body
is a wafer of itself, here
I am pitiful, not the striding city gal but
the timid green girl
my feet thin and dumb
I hold each breath until   it is clasped
to the next like hands
of kindergarten children crossing a street

when I listen, I'm afraid of what I might hear, if
I follow the sound of the chainsaw
will I find my father
will he hear me
over the sound of his cutting?
if I follow the scent of blackberries
will my mother be picking
her lard-pail full and tied to her waist?
and if she sees me, will she run spilling them
her eyes straining back like a startled deer?
and if she bolts, will I run after
bawling like her calf?
and if I lose sight of her
will I,   night
swell with your thickness or
dissolve in your black mouth?

I am five

when the needled-limbs loft and
blond grass-heads move like flames
I am five and
grasshoppers clack
snapping their hot wings
near my ear and
I am five
and breathing the body smell of this place
the skin of fruit-warm cedar, while
adolescent pines wrestle the wind;
they know everything
but I am five and
don't know that this burning inside is
loneliness

ghosted

a liquor-grin suspends him
past neon signs
down skid row streets
his shirt newly creased
his shoulders a yoke
for hauling
heavy saws and wedges
over windfalls, lifting chains, and
bucking logs

but this Saturday night he's clean-shaven
having crouched over a washbasin and
leaned his face into a small mirror
as one would into a kiss
to trim his moustache

and my mother is inflamed with jealousy
by his preening, by the women
who will drink with him, by
the way they look at my father

so frequently
she leaves him
where the women
and other Indians
drink, for she knows
the whiskey will loosen his anger
at the whiteman who is always boss
at his own cheap labour
at the money that never goes far enough

so he drinks
'til he doesn't remember
'til his new shirt drips from his belt
'til his grin folds cast-iron bitter

'til his spirit is sucked from his eyes, and
he is taken again
ghosted away
from the one who is my father
into a stranger, into an Indian
staggering down the street

the shape of water

the shape of water   between two limbs
is the proximity of siblings
knowing   the flinching
in each other's veins
on certain nights when
grown-ups
take the form of jackals
over a thin spot
in each other
isolate a yearling
from old vanities, the herd
in high grass
pins its body   the length of it
feels its life shiver
then feels nothing

the next morning
they are hangdog
and ponderous
like they didn't mean it
like tomorrow is another day
like the shape of water between two limbs
could be different

City View

Main & Hastings

I feel the city sweat
closeness and
the drift of urban indians
hot pavement, dried condoms, deals
Main and Hastings
city transit crowded with latinos, blacks
and asians down through the tunnel of trade
Daily I ride through foreign exchange of
skin for paper, paper for pills or powder
paper for cloth, cloth for sex and sex for power
This daily exchange for skin, for paper, for cloth, for power—
everything here can be bought or exchanged
Some things cannot be refunded

Powell

on the dull circuit
     to my day-job
     I try not to
     stare
     but my gaze is threaded
     to the needle-thin figures
     who live in doorways and
     streets I pass, benignly
     on the bus
the doorway shelters
     I quickly lose
     sight of, are: kitchen, den, garage, two and half
     baths to someone
     I splay open
     with my curiosity
     as if I were glancing at the 6 o'clock-
     somewhere-else-news
I shift in my seat watching
     stick figures hunt
     more rock, powder, or dust
     divine cement veins
     sift dirt and street litter
     for crystals
     for precious wonder

"the drive"

and the young sous-chef chops red pepper near my sleeve
a coffee comes between us
a thin blade away from each other
the twenty-something's and I
frequently meet like this
over the counter or cash
register in cafes, restaurants, and movie theatres

they serve me here too
at the Cafe-du-Because we know
we could be panning on the street in minus 10 Celsius
like the two young pierced, tattooed, and shivering skins
sitting a cardboard's thickness away from icy cement with
their CV's:
Homeless, Not on Welfare, Willing to Work
for Money

Robson

wouldn't it be tidy to think that this city cop and royal-blue redhead sipping coffee beside me were at fault for the two thin "streets" who scavenge nearby and wouldn't I be blameless if all it took to alter this divide were to dissuade the cop and the royal-blue redhead from buying two hundred thousand-dollar condos for the sake of the two thin bums who beg and fry on the concrete

Napier

workers are dragging home to supper and the cafes are empty:
the ceilings high, the fans apparent, the music filling the spaces
where the big-mouthed diners sat before guitar sounds echo
off eggshell walls, and the stacked tins of artichokes, tomatoes
and olive oil. now the ceiling fans clear out the day's chatter,
the coolers hum to themselves; and I watch the day's stragglers
lug their stretching bags home, and finally the street cools in
the memory of mothers & strollers, squeaky buses, ninety-nine
cent pizza diners and shaved, pierced and tattooed x-ers

Salsbury

Our breath hums us sometimes
inside out, tunes
our ribcage to the right pitch
after one whole breath
we are stirred enough to
shut off the alarm
grind the coffee
squeeze the toothpaste
lock the door
stop at corners
look both ways, walk
to the number 4, appear
at work for eight hours, retrace
our steps home, lock
the door behind us, feed
the cats, then ourselves, settle
back into our armchairs with
newspaper, magazine or television monitor

Oak

it's still, the buildings red and giving in to darkness. Lights come on in small windows. I imagine those insides to be warm and active with supper, a husband and wife and possibly children. Someone who says, "How was your day?" Face smiling, open and round as the frying pan, sausages nestled, lined up like warm piglets ready to suckle. I imagine the other removing his or her shoes and coat, setting down heavy bags and answering, "Fine." I imagine their four hands spreading out the tablecloth, a hand for each corner. I imagine the sound of cutlery being pulled from the drawer, the sound of lids being lifted from pots ready on the stove, the placing of bread and butter, salt, the water glasses, the steaming soup, love. I imagine the light from small windows

Hastings

the night sky is neon-blue darkening
at the same time illuminating
this near-summer evening
I sit quietly
resting, in the dissolving day while
outside electric buses pull movie-goers, bar-hoppers
junkies, lovers, and tourists along shoreless
Hastings
to the urban core and all around
the city hums and sirens and farts on religiously while
my neighbors behind paned glass are fused
to the flicker of cablevision

Terminal avenue

Friday night I ride the #14 home, and I realize too late that it is the last-call express. Patrons—wedged and talkative, smelling of beer, some angry, swearing, others "charmed"—everyone weaving to the marinade of some liquor or other while the hum of the electric lines pulls us home. In the din of drunken-ness, anger and frivolity someone claims that they have lost a "contact." The memory of sport's skirmishes rushes back to me, but no one here gets two minutes for elbowing. As is the custom on Vancouver City Transit, no one notices while one of the more unbalanced does the transit-weave in search of the ill-fated "contact." It is never found, like so many things lost in this city. My stop comes, and I brush past strangers' bodies smelling of sweat, beer and smoke, closer physically to some than I've been to a few lovers. The bus door opens, air like my breath rushes in and I am safely released to the street again

Broadway

I am now Hastings and Main, tattooed, pierced, shaved and dyed; the rain and rhododendrons and the Lion's Gate Bridge; I am now the panhandlers, the junkies, the hookers, the homeless, all of them, the Vancouver city transit, crowded and crabby, "the Drive," Film Festival and umbrellas, the lights of Grouse Mountain; I am now more city than I thought the Burrard shipyards and the nine o'clock gun; I am too, the disquieted waters of the Fraser, the factories and mills that fidget next to it; I am the ferry lineups, the plum tree blossoms in March, the green smog over Abbotsford, the blueberries, humidity, three weeks of rain, and grey sky on my raincoat

Gazing Ground

grazing grounds

the ghosts of deer graze on stubble in harvested fields while the sky overhead is cranberry-blood stained. they graze, spirits in a field while a mile away geese bed down, itinerants in stubble and lost grains of wheat. and there's a skin of ice lying in the ditches, and the blond grass bunches at the knees of the bone-bare poplar, all at dusk, pointing skyward

mirage

I'm beginning to settle like dust on a stretch of prairie road. It's August and the only thing breaking the heat is horizon. It's this equation I crave: earth under sky. Never sharper than on a hot day when a trail of dust from a farm truck disappears into pale heat. Wide openness, where I am left to compare grasses, their shade of green, the length and shape of their blades, or to look up and study the demeanor of clouds: some stretched like a skiff of snow across an iron field or others as big and threatening as bad tempers. There I am able to witness the dust rising from a farm truck miles away and consider it wondrous

nothing asks me to leave

I.

my back to the land

even though this is not my air   I breathe
not my water   I drink
nor ground I know   I impose
my footprint, for however long it stays   even
though this is an ocean and I sit by; it doesn't stop
breathing   nor the sky I walk under fall   nothing asks
me to leave, and   I'm here inhaling its intimate animal
smells   of rot and birth   facing the ocean wind   still
while the water licks around me. And I stand on
the shore, my back to the land;   I immigrate   to an
ocean bigger than the prairie.   How could anything be
bigger than the prairie?

II.

clearing of water and sky

I bring you here to see
that water, that clearing
of water and sky
give it time
those green waves could be grass
those mountains, beyond the foothills and
this sea gale could be a wind off the prairie

The Bow River, Shaganappi, and Sarcee Trails

I have come home from the dry light; the snow covered nude space and its glare in prairie light, the slush and vacant suburbs. There is no reason for a city to appropriate these grasslands, riverbanks and otherwise, flatness. No reason, no good reason whatsoever. There's just a trace of farming and ranching on the cuff of people boarding the city bus, the oil industry coin on others. The sight of the Bow River, Shaganappi and Sarcee trails, and the mirage—foothills beyond the "Stoneys." There are no seagulls on this checkerboard rolling out west to the Rockies nor east to the mythic Shield. There are no seagulls to wake me from my dream

Wapiti

somewhere dancers dance singing

barefoot on sun-powdered earth
having twisted prayers
in tobacco for others
each bright tie a sparrow that lifts
in a flock from the burning

somewhere dancers dance singing
while transit coins fall
and you gaze out of that moment of leaves
between a refinery and a gas station
while the shadows cut lace on your flank
through an instant of salal and limbs
you look up from grazing
and I leave bills and overdraft
just long enough to register
silence

along a sequence of storefronts
and scheduled stops I think of cold
and hunger
how you kept us from it

your generous hide stretching over ours
while others prized only your head
hung above billiard tables

and still others called you relative
and strung your slate hooves
from their rattles in dance

somewhere dancers dance singing
in colours of their breath
without food or drink
while the sun burns their shadow to the ground

and those who dance for me
are dying of thirst
while the sweet curve of your face, wapiti
restores that sleeve of me
faithless as driftwood
and just as ashen

while somewhere   dancers dance singing

Mine Fields

green girl dreams Mountains

I was a green girl then
round-eyed and hardly hurt
when I knew these mountain friends

And there's a sun's blade
on Cypress mountain's greenness
cut through
to that time of the round-eyed girl
in me when
I rode horses along the mud flats
of the Columbia River
with some ready-sweet boys
and a boyfriend whose hair
was the color of corn silk
My breasts were weasels' noses
my hips narrow and firm
In those days my body
volunteered me, pulled me
onward to dreams, verdant
and monumental

naked wind

I remember a time in July when
he and I lay under a willow tree;
the heat pressed down and a breeze brushed
our arms and legs
as we lay on a thin blanket
spread on the fragrant grass; I remember tasting
his lips, savoring his sweat, and feeling the heat
trace through
my seams like liquor, melting to my groin
until I wanted to undress and ride him in the naked wind

mine fields

I'm so relieved
that one look

between us now
can say that much

when a year ago
we were just having trouble with sentences

let alone glances
as we quarreled and

it took days to decipher
by phone and sometimes

the occasional note to negotiate
the minefields of wounds laid down previously

having said nothing, yet

     1.

Fern fronds, warm rain
so unlike December on the plains   I remember
space so open you could walk out and never come back
my stance, the only interruption
on a surface so flat you could
if your arm would reach
run your hand over the surface of it like a table
a surface somewhat like the sea, you know
and cast your eyes out over it in the way of your father
Have you ever wanted   to gaze out as far as your eyes could
take you and never come back?
Have you, my darling   ever wanted to
understand the prairie in me   like I
want to understand   the sea in you?

2.

The way you describe sweet
makes me think of pleasure
drawn out taut as   a violin string
and plucked   just once
so that the memory
of the note taking up space   is more real than
the note struck   inside us

"Sweet," you say
like it comes in jars
and we only remember tasting
because it never lasted long

3.

And yet there is more I want   to say
having said nothing, yet
I have imbibed it   more than once   you
never have tasted it

burn, blaze now

1.

It was a grand turning in our lives   two women awakening
with red-ore veins   we almost became the unspeakable   in
our terror   our changing   today, after seeing you again   I
am a sack of kittens dropped in dark liquid, filling   drained
hour-glass like by: "Cherokee Louise," a song   memory of a
time we both trembled from body violation sores   our interi-
ors were open gullies we bled into and the blood collected in
carnelian pools

2.

our hair trailed us then in the prairie wind, the same   wind
that slanted the bronze wheat heads under a sky that promised
this was when we were wrapped in the blue-gauze of our hori-
zons   and migrated separately   from the planed land that
stood us   you turned South, after the same intoxication as
O'Keeffe   the desert-blessed   those with lesions and deceased
mothers   to picture the smooth sanding   I faced west   to the
end of prairie & land   saw the tangle of rainforest green in my
desires   set to clearing a space in its thick undergrowth   write
myself upright once more   while sea-waves witnessed my raw-
ness

3.

after four years   a spirit lights upon me in my sleep   a crisp
truth   we: the one turning south, the one facing west   came
through slaughter   passed through the asshole of institutions
the scrutiny of white yardsticks   the rebuke of ourselves   "we
(who) were never meant to survive"   burn, blaze now   like
firebrand

" A Litany for Survival," Audre Lorde

scorching

1.

Scorching sun and my
                    desire
                              hotter than the red tips
of the burning bush
out my window

2.

I settle in a chair
          glowing
in full sunlight and
assflower
melts open
       into its hands
                imagined mouth
cupping my nectar

3.

I wait
      and wait
              and
                    wait

for my young lover
to be at my door
his smile sweet

as the pinkness
of his mouth, his
teeth white
        lashes curved and
                waiting
                    for me to
                            lick
them in the door

4.

I hold
        desire
            kindle it, carry
        one coal
                lit
into the next day

lover

I would like to feast on your nipples
taste the heat of your skin
lift your curved black
lashes with my tongue
lick them lightly until
the tingle ripples down your stalk
blossoming in your stamen

pastries

I miss that you
brought me
pastries
placed them
secretly
at my door
so that I came home to
a small white manila box
wrapped with purple ribbon
and inside
sweet flaky tart crust
filled with lemon meringue or
almond paste
feeding your way
to my heart

the stain

I dreamt of ripe flowers
        that drew me to their lips
                I lifted one head to discover
    blackberries
    nested beneath
                  roe-swollen and yearning
          and as I reached for one nipple
              a sheet of honeyed beads
                rose in my hand
like latticework
I hoarded their buds in greed
        'til I noticed a patch
           that writhed like maggots
              with pustules clustered in
black jelly and juice fluxing over blisters
I recoiled my hand
        but my fingers were stained
              and the stain was veritable

              and familiar

a sorry slackening

We said we'd pick blackberries
said we'd sleep out under the longest day
that we'd hike
I said I'd take more pictures
read more books, exercise
and that I'd meditate
sew and
pray

now the leaf has turned   the berries are over and
these are the warm last days
loosening to the leaving light and

                              yellow cooling
this another darkening, turning inward we try
assure ourselves of greenings
other berries   other turnings

wrapping the bundle of my dream of you

I am wrapping the bundle of my dream   of you   one frame at a time one line at a time of your exquisite face   you sailed to North America on   I am wrapping the bundle of your face one leaf of skin on another   I am wrapping   the bundle of your face   layering it   sheaf after sheaf of bright cloth   scarves tissue of taste   touch   sound   smell of bodysalt   sweet taste of cardamom   on your bodyhair   soft clean curryhair   I am bundling your face away   I am wrapping the bundle of your face away   I am carrying the bundle of your presence, now   I am cradling the bundle of your face   I am walking the bundle of your body to its place, now I am carrying the bundle of your face to its end   of my horizon, my vision   to its place, its resting   I am watching the light change in my heart for you I am watching the light fade in my hand for you, I am watching the light dissolve in my hands for you, I am watching . . .

"'Wrapping the bundle,' is a South Korean expression, which signifies a transition from one life-stage to another." Soo-Ja Kim, South Korean Artist

Among the Word Animals

word swarm

word animal sounds come
in waking, in broad day-
light the night
is uncovered by the day
a heavy patched quilt thrown off and
all these starry-eyed gestures
and willow bark-bit
eyelids, chewed like birch bark bees
mosquitoes and horse flies
from the mouth
of Angelique swarm

Angelique Merasty of Amisk, Manitoba, now deceased, was famed in the world as a birch bark-biting artist. She passed on her art to Angelique Levac of Prince George, British Columbia, who presently practices it. "Birch Bark Biting is an ancient art form once commonly practiced by northern Woodland women. It is produced by finding the proper piece of bark and separating it into layers. The innermost layer is folded and refolded and then bitten into to produce intricate designs. Birch Bark Bitings were originally used as patterns for bead and quillwork designs."

solo

Saturday morning single
crows break through
morning fog
and traffic sounds bow
trees in a slow motion rehearsal
other black flitting birds dot "i's" and place quotation
marks around
a lone seagull's squall
while I and others fumble
toward coffee, our sleepy feet brushing
the carpet and tile in some mute jazz percussionist's solo

sound shard

rectangular blocks
of sound, blocks of why
do our voices collide
in the often fragile air?
frigid and crackling,
sound circles our legs, shoulders, and
ears. what are the notes
we draw from to remedy ourselves?
notes we shave from each other
scrape these broken tones off my breasts
scrape every last shard of a shape like grief
fear, and dread until I shine
shave the f's for they frighten me
shave the e's for they rip my skin like fishhooks, then
drag me along into darkness

birdnote

his spirit is asleep but birds wake me
in the four-directions-hour and
talk to me in *a language*. It isn't a language
with syllables or vowels, its keys—
each bone is a note in the throat
carried so far you can still
hear their panting from the flight
each bird carrying—
and that note can't
be sounded until the note before it
is sounded, the note before it is sounded

sad flute

sad, sadness hangs inside me
like clothes on someone
who has suddenly lost weight
grayness inside my ribcage
flaps in the wind through me
the numb hole that someone could play a tune through
if they were big enough and could hold me sideways
like God or someone
if they could hold my stiff body
like a shiny flute and blow a mighty wind
through

reed instrument my body
woodwind my larynx
the keys of a clarinet
lifting open and shut
its sweet hollow sound echoing
a reed for God or some other mad musical
inclination to play a ditty or dirge on my losses

stillness for company

1.

I want a man who   knows the meaning
of stillness
who sits beside it   and holds its hand
looks into its eyes   who feels loneliness
and doesn't run   who sees stillness
and doesn't rock   the boat, who smells
a cold, wet wind   feels its sting and sees
in it clarity, I   want a man who knows
his own name   in the noise of that same
wind, someone   who goes to the water's
edge for company

2.

I want to settle in   stillness, settle in
quiet and wake   to nothing more
than the sound   of wind
in the clock   of the trees

3.

And I want   to share that still-
ness with   someone who
has learned   his own

still

to be still, to truly be
still, to be still and reflect

for a change,   the clouds move past
listen to the wind.   I imagine
the ocean grey and rocky
the wind gusting fresh
restless and raw, raw and pulling
spring behind it like a sibling
on a sleigh after a day of sledding

roll

remember when   the summer sun   dried the streets and there
was the sound of kids playing   in some park and the cars had
their windows rolled down and their radios on   remember the
excitement, the anticipation of summer only it's spring and
the wind is as restless as a gambler

raw

     1.

raw sunshine of day-
lightness   smell of cut grass
lemon on the tongue
raw light of night   coming forward
cool green   dank smell of hidden animals
birds and worms   leaf-mold

     2.

split wood
my chest and belly
like kindling fall
to the side of the raw light

     3.

this cut   rawness
of grass   sunshine
descent of blood
into night
a return   open flowing

bright beads

"I am a cluster of bright beads" in snow
perfectly round glistening berries
salmon egg-transparent
bubbles breaking honey-sweet
pomegranate seeds in the tiny shell of my mouth
juice-berry and cedar-smelling
pine perfect greening
hills where they nested like partridges
in the grass and needles damp
as the soft warm peeking sun
in spring, in spring

"I am a feather on the bright sky," N. Scott Momaday

"dawn always begins in the bones"

and ends in the heart
my love
I love you like
the crocus the spring air
the light rippling over slopes
the rolling hills rising and falling
as if light on their uneven ground had weight

"dawn always begins in the bones" and
through the day filters
like silt through water
gathering cloudily into pools of night once again

"dawn always begins in the bones" and
ends in the dust of wagons
on their return to deliver suns west and
the wagons wake us while our dreams stream
gone by like bright scarves of dust
drawn out by the wind in their passing

"Hymn to Ra," from *Awakening Osiris: The Egyptian Book of the Dead*, translated by Normandi Ellis.

birds pin it down

the limbs and leaves of trees inhale light and
exhale   night's coolness
settles in and birds
pin it down
with their beaks
for the next ten hours
before eyelids pull it back
to day

I give you arbutus

I give you this
place, secret in the garden
flowering vulvas, host-
white tulips and lipstick tube
buds penetrating the shy evening
I give you the sand smooth arbutus
proud dogwood collars
laughing yellow vines and
the cool hollow of the earth
descending day. I give you
the brush of cool fronds, light
tails trailing through dark cedars and
the breath of blossom

arbutus I

Now the arbutus is raining   its skin
                    crackling like wood sap catching fire
                    snapping to life, and
        the evening's resting, cooling
                    makes its skin contract   as if it were
                molting, excitedly breaking away from its
bindings

arbutus II

sky scorches blue while
arbutus split their dresses
pull me into their smooth lime arms

dried stigmas of crocus

float on remembering
it's evening or half-day
light, the air clear
the evening's hood is that slate blue
it's brisk and you're walking home
the snow on the mountain radiates light while
the ocean harbours night
the sun soaks the roofs of houses
the color of saffron and yellow onion skins
but it's cold and here, not
desert as the sun's colouring would have you
believe and you wish you were there and
here in this cold
yet as this day departs
you know it's holy
and needs to be addressed
in the way that the stirring inside
of you wants to slow waltz
as she, the evening
leaves the dance floor
and you float on remembering
her steps inside you

up/write

the image of
her sweet body held
in her mother's arms
lifts like an ink separation of
black, white and grey
   the Holy Ghost leaving or
   is it returning?
and it's the grey she's used to
the black and white she's never been able to fathom, but
she lifts off the page
and her tiny face drifts up

her spirit translucent as the glass on the shower stalls in
other-people's-homes, or
rice paper she saw once, in Chinatown,   20 years ago
she was always drawn to rice paper,   after that
to its whiteness,   like communion hosts

if you held her spirit up to the light, the light
would flow through her fine center
and the light did
and people used to say to her "If a big wind came along?"
what if a big wind did come along?
where would she have landed?
upright, I guess
she knew she had more than one life

her first life she misplaced 'til age 39
the time, gone like the air in a vacuum
a black hole of memory
another life she lost at age two
wading into a swift river behind her older siblings and
regained it on the same banks of that river
spewing water
like a cherub in an English garden
her brothers and sisters using her arms like wings
to pump the water out

still another she lost at age four
rolling down Snake Hill in front of a boulder
that chose her out of a crowd
of rodeo fans   worshipping danger

she seemed to attract death

and now at forty, would she choose
once more, in her slow revolution
of turning   Right   Side   Up
to land on all four posts of her being
or would she follow the last ghost of a life
time running out, like her the year she finally said, "Enough,
I'm fed up with trying to please every tom, dick and jane?"
"What is it? What is it I am supposed to do?" And the voice
that came back said, "Write"
and she knew that she had landed
once more
up/write

grammar boot camp

I come to this day of writing empty
handed not a thief of the night's
wanderings or the day's promise
I come empty, I have locked
the cats out and me in
I've successfully made my cup of coffee without words
not a preposition to speak of, and
I'm ready
I come to this keyboard without
words and hope
that I will find some
fallen through the cracks
through the keys
from one of those days
when I had more
to say than I had time or
when I had more
words than sense or typing speed

I come empty after a week of chalk dust
repeating myself   and students who come in late
empty, just the thought of run-ons, fragments
and insubordination

Straw Boss

I strut the glassy classroom floor in ink black cowboy boots for
I am the English teacher in a classroom of Sioux, Saulteaux and
Cree speakers; I am the head honcho grammarian riding the
range looking to lasso comma splices, cut fragments away from
the herd, corral faulty logic, run-ons, and brand incorrect sub-
ject-verb agreement: XSV. I am the straw boss in a stable of
grammatical errors and I'm gonna break those wild ponies and
turn them into the sweetest little filly sentences you'd ever cinch
a saddle on

blond syllables

those blue-eyed, long-lashed sentences or the green-eyed
verbs and auburn adjectives, and those Oh! Oh! sun-burned
bikini strap exclamation marks, peaches-n-cream commas
and powdered nose, pockless, prefixes and little tight-assed
suffixes make me want to swear a red fuckin' Cree streak

"blond syllables of English." Tim Seibles

throatsong to the four-leggeds

but slowly
we sniff each other's airs, noses flare
jaws drop to the shape of "O"
in the mouth
then"Ahhh"
in the throat
the other wind instrument
and we suck and blow
volley the air between us
through a long dark throatshaft
back and forth, back
and forth, through
a song travelling now
from my throat to your
call and response
call
and response to the windpipe opening and
closing the sound of elk whistling
the vibrations of moose throttle through nasal passages
stretching
back into the gut of ancestors, sucking and mewling
deer, moose in the muscle of our being
back into the ancestors we are

back into groin of our helplessness now
into the rhythm of our joy and pain
freedom to move back and forth, between and
over the pine needles of space
push through the cool dimness of spruce, fir and maybe cedar
back to the song of wind in the limbs of space
your space and mine now
in this era of animal tracks
in the muskeg pungent earth mixed
with droppings of ourselves and
we climb the limbs of being
into the past of bawling animals
in the bush we once hunted for their generous red-blue flesh
that fed us even through our own wanting and neglect
we ate all the sweetmeat of those animals
then sucked the bones white
that became our whistles when we danced and
the crosses when we prayed
in the Lake of St Anne and
all our sisters who gave us mercy when
we wouldn't grant it to ourselves
our bodies old
in recognition of what was gifted us
from those four-leggeds that mewl
far back in memory of a world
that was forever bigger and vaster than any of us

I am thankful to have eaten
from those beasts that feed even me
now in my occasional starvation song
I do remember it sometimes, but
only fleetingly behind shyness that hums
through my nose and larynx
the tune of animal remembrances
and single notes of gratitude
for those mammals that sustained me even
before I could mewl myself in my mother's belly
the chord that she struck was the chord that bore
both of us through all those times of want and waste
of breath that we never put to good use
in song or bellowed back refrain
of gutsong and throatsong to our relatives
now in our days of plenty

About the Author

Marilyn Dumont is of Cree/Metis ancestry. Since 1985, she has published in numerous Canadian literary journals, and her work has been widely anthologized, as well as broadcast on radio and television. Her first collection of poems—*A Really Good Brown Girl* —won the 1997 Gerald Lampert Memorial Award from the League of Canadian Poets. She has taught Creative Writing at Simon Fraser University and Kwantlen University-College in Vancouver. She has also worked in video production as an intern with the National Film Board. She holds an MFA from the University of British Columbia, and was most recently Writer-In-Residence at the University of Alberta.